CHEERS FROM THE SIDELINES

"I have worked alongside Coach for almost 10 years, as he facilitates my camp in California. Recently I came to observe the Playmakers After-School Program and I was so impressed. Coach's program is facilitated by college-age student athletes who are teaching 'old school' accountability, character and values, which our young kids desperately need for a strong foundation.

"Playmakers is creating leadership opportunities and peer-to-peer mentoring in a very unique way. These young third through sixth graders are doing things that we can all be proud of. Playmakers is using sports as a tremendous tool for life lessons. I am a Playmakers supporter, all the way."

—*Tim Brown, 2015 Pro Football Hall of Fame,*
Tampa Bay Buccaneers, LA/Oakland Raiders,
Notre Dame Wide Receiver, 1987 Heisman Trophy Winner,
1987 Walter Camp Award, 2009 College Football Hall of Fame

"I first met Coach Greg Roeszler my freshman year of high school when I tried out for football. Now I was no star athlete. In fact, as a young boy, I dealt with several physical challenges. The doctors told my parents that I would never walk without braces on my legs. With God's help, I was able to overcome these difficulties. Coach Roz and football played an important role in helping me do that.

"Despite my lack of athleticism or apparent value as a football player, Coach Roz was committed not only to make me a better football player, but also to make me a better person. There were days when I felt like quitting football. On those days, he would tell me, 'Hey Buddy, if you quit, I quit.' His belief in me helped me believe in myself. He showed me that I was capable of more than I thought I was, or more than my circumstances should have allowed.

"Over my life, Coach Roz has remained a close friend and mentor. I have had the opportunity to be part of the birth and growth of the Playmakers organization. Being a Playmaker helped prepare me for my future as a pastor in the Church of the Nazarene. I will always be grateful to Coach Greg Roeszler and Playmakers for the impact they had, and continue to have, on my life."

—*Pastor Andrew Murakami, Willows, California*

"It was football and, more than that, my relationship with Coach Roz, that saved me. I don't know if he knows it or not, but those endless hours on one hundred yards of grass were therapy for a knucklehead who didn't know how to express what was going on in his world. I am eternally grateful for our relationship that hasn't faded over time or distance. Thank you, Coach. You are the hero, not me. I am just a guy serving his country, and I am proud to do so, especially with people like you who understand the sacrifice."
—*Ensign Jason Martz, US Navy, Sacramento, California*

"Donna Miesbach is a very accomplished writer. She obviously has a passion for athletics and a great knowledge of the sport of football. I found her writing ability to be exceptional and believe that anyone interested in athletics will value her books."
—*Tom Osborne, Athletic Director, University of Nebraska*

"Greg, I'm so proud of you for being such a difference maker at Encina. You're part of the select few who realize that winning and losing is WHAT YOU DO, while exhibiting good sportsmanship and outstanding character is WHO YOU ARE. Many years from now these guys will come back and thank you for teaching them to be disciplined and to walk in integrity. No matter how tough it gets this season, keep your head up and remember the REAL reason you're coaching. God bless you, Roz. I believe in you!!"
—*Scott Sorgea, former High School Athletic Director, Sacramento, California*

My hat is off to you, as you work to inspire and encourage and teach this game, which may be the only 'rite of passage' left in America. It is so important for our young men to adopt an attitude of hard work, courage, sacrifice, determination and maturity before entering adulthood. It is just as important for young men to recognize their improvements and build on them. Keep up the good work, and keep in touch. Go Bulldogs!"
—*Jeffrey "Skip" Thompson, Former Hermiston High School Football Coach and current seminarian, Hermiston, Oregon*

"Wow! What a tremendous day we had with you and Donna on Tuesday! The news of your coaching session with our staff has traveled to the far reaches of both of our campuses. Everyone is talking about 'Roz.'"
—*Tracy Wells, Director of Donor Relations,*
Uta Halee Home for Girls, Omaha, Nebraska

"To know Coach Roz and to be a Playmaker has been the best thing that could happen to inner city kids. We love you, Coach Roz."
—*Lorenzo Walsh, Coach and Director,*
Sacramento Jr. Falcons Youth Football, South Sacramento, California

"You're an inspiration. Never stop what you are doing."
—*Kari, Student at a Group Home, Omaha, Nebraska*

"Beyond his skills as a football coach, Greg Roeszler has a genuine passion for instilling values of character and discipline in the hearts of the athletes under his charge."
—*Mark Ludwig, a player's dad, Sacramento, California*

"Coach Roz is one of the greatest men I know, as well as one of my heroes. All who come in contact with him end up better men and better football players."
—*Tony Gillespie, former student athlete, San Jose, California*

"At a speech to the student body last spring, our son spoke of this amazing coach who had no reservations about extending acceptance to someone who didn't feel capable of doing very much. Coach Roz will forever be the person Andrew holds up as one who truly made a difference in his life."
—*Bette Murakami, a player's parent, Rancho Cordova, California*

"I would like to personally thank whoever was in charge of bringing Mr. Roeszler out to our Agency. He was phenomenally amazing! What a battery charger!!!!! My heart burned the entire time I was listening to him. I want to be doing more hands-on work with kids and am praying about it. Thank you, thank you for such a fine gift."
—*Lana Kowalski, Secretary, Uta Halee Home for Girls, Omaha, Nebraska*

"Roz, you are an amazing person. I admire what you do for people who aren't lucky enough to have their own opportunities. Your coming here opened my eyes to what some other people don't have. I believe that Playmakers can go anywhere. I hope you come back and visit us."

—*Maribelle, Student at a Group Home, Omaha, Nebraska*

"Donna did an amazing job helping Greg write the books. She had me in tears at times."

—*Coach Chris Berg, Oak Park, California,*
www.CoachChrisBerg.com, Sacramento, California

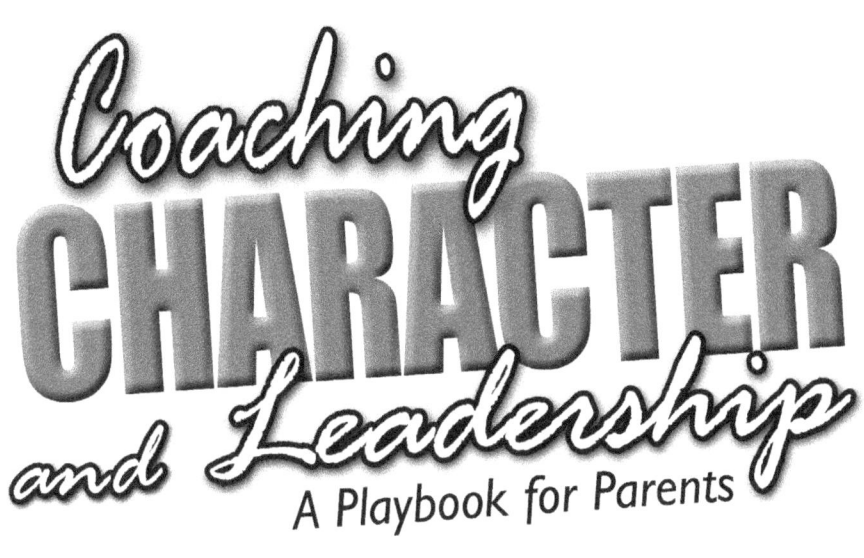

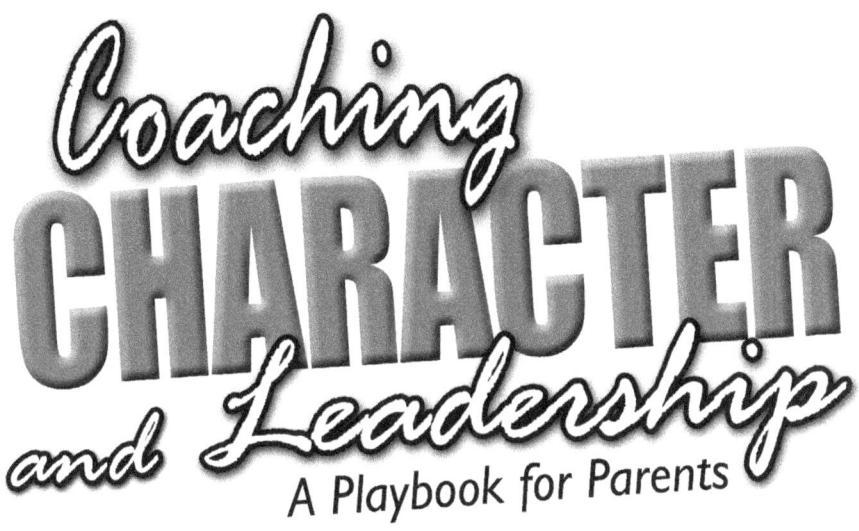

Coaching CHARACTER and Leadership
A Playbook for Parents

Greg "Coach Roz" Roeszler
with Donna Miesbach
Foreword by David Humm

Folsom, California

© 2017 Greg Roeszler and Donna Miesbach. All rights reserved. No part of this book may be used or reproduced in any manner whatsoever without written permission except in the case of brief quotations embodied in critical articles or reviews. Any similarities to other intellectual works are either coincidental or have been properly cited when the source is known. Trademarks of products, services, and organizations mentioned herein belong to their respective owners and are not affiliated with Playmakers Press.

The names of some of the students mentioned in this book have been changed. Their stories have not.

On the back cover: Playmakers Free Summer Football Camps are for children ranging in age from seven to nineteen. Each year some child emerges who touches your heart in a special way. These kids become Coach Roz's helper and get a shoulder ride throughout the camp. The shoulder rides began when the little boy in this picture didn't want to stay. He felt overwhelmed by how many children were there and told Coach Roz he'd really rather go home. Roz picked the boy up and put him on his shoulders. That helped a little, but he still wasn't sure he wanted to stay, so Roz made him an Assistant Coach and gave him jobs to do. From that point on, the boy loved the camp and stayed all three days.

ISBN13: 978-0-9822514-4-7
Cataloging in Publication Data on file with publisher.

Playmakers Press
A Division of Playmakers Mentoring Foundation
2795 E. Bidwell St, Suite 100
Folsom, CA 95630
(916) 220-1284
E-mail: CoachRoz@ThePlaymakers.org

Editorial Services: Donna Miesbach
Marketing & Publicity: Concierge Marketing, Inc.

Printed in the United States of America
10 9 8 7 6 5 4 3 2 1

Contents

Acknowledgments .... *xiii*
Foreword *1*
Introduction *3*

GRADES

Let's Work Together *7*
How Much Time Is Left? *9*
Take Pride in Your Grades *11*

GIRLS

What Does Coach Have to Say About Girls? *15*
Step Up and Be There! *17*
When to Let Go *19*
Treat Girls with Respect *21*

OUR JOB IS TO CARE FOR EACH OTHER

His Heart Is Not Too Small *25*
Fill Them Up! *27*
I Owe Pop Everything *29*
Healing Their Wounds *31*

HEROES

You Are Being Sent *35*
Hummer and Other Heroes *37*

CONDUCT

Laugh and Cry Every Day *41*
Way Beyond the Game *43*
Look Me in the Eye and Tell Me What Happened *45*
I Care About Your Character *47*
Hold Them Accountable. We Do. *49*
Love Them Harder *51*
You Can Play Through It *53*
"I'll Try" Won't Get It Done *55*
Let's Be Decisive *57*
It's All About Character *59*
In Conclusion *61*

COME JOIN US

Partnering with Playmakers *65*
Invite Coach Roz to Speak to Your Group *67*
Coaching for Character Clinics *69*
Playmakers' Free Summer Sports Camps *71*
About Playmakers' Books *73*
Order Form *75*
About the Authors *77*

Dedication

Especially to those single Moms who fight the good fight by themselves, thank you for allowing me to be a voice in helping you.

To my Mom, who is always there, and is my biggest fan.

Acknowledgments

As a young college student athlete, I have memories of coming home and going with my dad to his Lions Club meetings. With great pride he would introduce me as a future Heisman Trophy Winner (not to be). Then we would get up early on Saturday morning to go into the community and serve others with his civic group.

His lessons formed my heart to serve in the community. Today I have partnered with some tremendous organizations—Optimists, Rotary, Soroptimists, Kiwanis, and more. These selfless organizations helped shape me, and I will always be grateful. I admire these big-hearted people whose generosity has helped my kids in so many ways.

Our mentoring program has evolved so much over the past few years. As we have grown, we have realized that we must develop relationships with the kids at an earlier age to help them with the foundation they need. Even though our After-School Program is in its infancy, it is addressing that challenge.

We do that through character development, reading, sports, and recreation. These elements are delivered daily by trained college student athletes who are committed to providing character-based mentoring to our young kids.

As our young third through sixth graders watch college-age mentors model the principles of community service and leadership, they begin to understand our "Pay It Forward" philosophy. They can tell you what a value is, and what Playmakers' values are. They know what civic organizations, such as Optimists and Rotary, are. I am proud to be a member of these organizations.

Playmakers' formula is quite simple. Coach or teach with state-of-the-art technology, with the best mentor-coaches available, and then provide tremendous incentives to our kids for their best performance. While we are having great success, we continue to partner with heart-based organizations who look for better ways to get the job done. We believe that the best is yet to come.

So this book shows what a community can do to make a difference. It began with my team of Donna and Hummer, my church, and my family, who believed in what is possible. My Board is a tremendous group of people who guide me daily. My small group of guys, who I have met with on Saturday mornings for years, have prayed and supported me in so many ways. Then there are Jason Martz, Andrew Murakami, Jordan Richards, and my brother, Jeff, who have always had my back. My Pastors, Kent Carlson and Mike Lueken, both put the wind in my sails and kept my compass pointed in the true direction. It was my Pastors' direction and guidance that ultimately got me here. To my wife, Linda, who I will love and thank forever for letting me chase this.

And finally, this is all about the kids, those we have met and helped, and those we have not yet met. To all of you, I am eternally grateful.

—*Coach Roz*

Foreword

In this life and time of 500 television channels, with the internet and instant messaging, with new lifestyle magazines and old-style newspapers, there is no shortage of places to go for information.

But what if the subject is as simple as: What do I do for, or say to, my young daughter or son who is intent on playing sports? What do I say to support and inspire them? How can I teach them the things I want them to get out of that experience? How can they learn "life lessons" about following the rules, and teamwork, and what that word really means? How will they know what it means to be part of a team where they can learn how to win AND lose, and do both gracefully?

This book, written by my dear friend and former teammate, Greg "Coach Roz" Roeszler, is THE book I would want any mother OR father to read who didn't play sports and is struggling to help their child.

I am honored to write this foreword for my friend, and am even more humbled after having read his final draft. Roz has explained every situation that you're going to face, and put it in a way you can understand so you will be able to explain it to your son or daughter. This is going to bring you and your child together, and will help you both to connect and enjoy sharing this incredibly special time together.

Friend, I am honored you asked me to do this. Now I am going to share your book with my 18-year-old daughter and ask her if it would have helped her more if Dad had used "Coach Roz's techniques" with her when she was growing up.

—David Humm, Oakland/LA Raiders,
Buffalo Bills and Baltimore Colts 1975-1984

Introduction

As the founder of Playmakers Mentoring Foundation, I'd like to welcome you to our world. Our goal is to give at-risk kids a road map for a better way of life. Playmakers assists children through our after-school mentoring, sports, and character development programs, like the Let's Go Learn interactive multi-level computer-based reading course that is both fun and manpower efficient.

Since most of our kids have challenging home situations where reading resources are not available, working with this program not only boosts their self-confidence, they are actually starting to enjoy reading.

My role is that of a mentor, a high school football coach, and father. God has blessed me with two beautiful daughters, Katie and J.T., and my wonderful wife, Linda, who has given me the freedom to pursue my passion, which is reaching out to at-risk kids through the medium of coaching. The two things that wake me up in the middle of the night are lost kids and their lack of a positive role model in their young lives.

When a man is lucky enough to chase the larger story of his life, he is blessed. That is me. I get to work with a collection of lost kids who, over the years, have become part of our "family" by being Playmakers.

Coaching has taught me that the power and influence the right coach has on an entire family extends far beyond the football field. It affects the family long after their son or daughter has graduated from high school.

Over the years, I have collected quotes that I have either made up or "borrowed." At my age, I have forgotten which I have created and which I have copied from someone who influenced me. If you're reading this and I've used one of your quotes, please let me know. I'll be sure to give you the credit in the next printing.

I have shared these quotes with many single parents who have the next-to-impossible task of raising kids alone. As time has gone by, a growing number of parents have trusted me and given me the honor of having a voice in their family and with their sons. That is a privilege beyond words.

This book is a collection of some of my favorite quotes and advice that these Moms have liked. I've tried to expound on them in the hope that they will be useful to you and your child also.

Even though the majority of my work with Playmakers and as a head coach is with football players who have single moms, please know that these values apply across all family situations and for both male and female students. Where I've said "mom," you may apply "dad" or "grandma". Where I write about a male football player, you can apply that to your female volleyball player, or your child in the marching band. The important values will shine through no matter what your specific situation is, and the character-building will work just as well for you.

My hope and prayer is that our organization of Playmakers can help moms and dads build young people of character. I know firsthand that the right coach at the right time can change the trajectory of a kid who just needs to have a man who can be trusted on his side.

—*Coach Roz*

Action Point:

You can be a Playmaker, too.
Use these tips with your family.

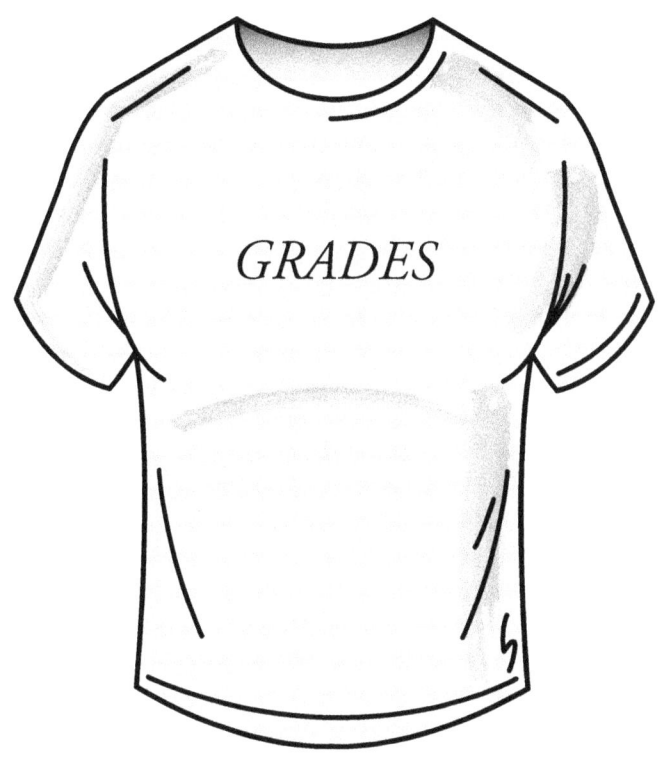

Let's Work Together

I believe that one of my jobs as coach is to help your son keep his priorities in proper order. With your support, I can help keep him on track. Allow me to be a voice in your family. If you believe that I am more concerned with his progress as a young man than as a fullback, we can get the job done together. You can trust me. If we have met, if we have discussed this philosophy and are developing a relationship, then together we are forming a "coaching staff" for your son.

The teachers are part of our football staff. Your son needs to know that the algebra teacher has as much authority as his line coach. I make it clear to your son that his teacher-coach is part of our football team. We work together. The first question that I ask the teacher (in front of your son) is, "Is this player giving you his best effort?" It all begins right there.

At Encina High School, where I am the head football coach, football begins at 6:45 in the morning at our study program where all of our kids get their homework out of the way first. Did you know that most teachers are on campus at that hour? Your son can get to school and get some individual help early in the morning. What kind of message does it send if your son is there EARLY to improve in the classroom? Teachers really do want to help your son. By going this extra mile to get it done, we send a message to Administration that we are serious about grades being first.

Good grades do not happen by accident. That is why we have a plan to help your son with his grades. By the way, none of my players have a driver's license yet. Our kids ride public transportation, walk, or ride bikes to get to school. They find a way to get there.

So where do girlfriends come in? THIRD. They happen after your son has met the girlfriend's dad. That's right. I tell our boys, "Go introduce yourself to her dad, look him in the eye, and shake his hand. Ask him what the rules are, and then behave as though you were dating Coach's daughter." Every football player understands that this is probably NOT the girl he is going to marry, and she is not his whole universe. If your son needs to talk to someone about this—and he usually does, whether he knows it or not—he can talk to Coach. Coach can give him a perspective that mom may not have. Ask Coach to get involved and talk to your son. It will create a relationship that is valuable to all.

If some guy shows up at my house to meet me, he has been "coached" by my daughter on what I want to know. He won't have a hat, skull cap or do-rag on. (I am "old school.") He will introduce himself, give me a handshake that I understand, and tell me where he goes to school. He will tell me about his college plan, and he'd better at least fake being interested in making an impression on me. I tell you this because that is what I teach my players as well. That is how we roll.

ACTION POINT:

Post your goals on the fridge.
Put the report card on the fridge.

How Much Time Is Left?

Our players understand the game of football. You might not think so, as I have just taken over a team that has lost thirty-six games in a row. So it would probably be more accurate to say, "We are learning to understand the game of football."

When a player is having trouble with grades, I ask him, "What is the score (your current grade), and how much time is left?" Just like in a game, we need to know these things. By knowing how much time is left, we can then put together a "game plan" for the rest of the game. This means going to the teacher and finding out exactly what needs to be done to win the game. How do we get the assignments current, and who is going to be his study coach?

Encina football players are "coached" on where to sit—or where to ask to be seated—the first day of class. I may be an old guy, but I know that the GPAs (grade point average) of the people in the front of the class are better than the GPAs in the back. I know where it is more fun to sit because, when I was in school, I sat back there, too. My players ask to sit up front because they know that by doing so, they show they are serious about school. Does this mean you can't get good grades in the back? No, it just means that we want to make a statement that we are more interested in seeing the board than we are about "being cool" in the back. If the teacher seats students alphabetically, then ask him or her to call your son "a student athlete."

The first week of school is critical to the tempo your son is going to set. We need to set a tempo that will stay with him all year. This means that if he will just carry books, sit up front and not be a pain to the teacher the first week, he may get the reputation of being a good guy. So many kids get "labeled" by the teacher early on because they needed to make a statement that they were the funniest, the coolest, or needed attention by giving the teacher a hard time the first week.

I expect my kids to show up ready for practice the first week. Our players have backpacks that say, "STUDENT ATHLETE." The backpacks have become very popular. More importantly, they make a statement on campus about what comes first, and what is most important to the football family.

As a coach, I ask the players to "catch our eye," meaning let us see you doing something well on the field. The same rule applies in the classroom: catch the teacher's eye by DOING THE RIGHT THING! As players, we like the attention we get when we catch the coach's eye. Remember, your son's teachers are coaches. The people in Administration are coaches, too. Teachers talk to each other. Opinions (good and bad) are reinforced every day. We all need to catch someone's eye by doing the right things.

ACTION POINT:

Know your child's school schedule.
What is their "toughest" class?
What is that teacher's name?

Take Pride in Your Grades

Mom, your son needs to understand that his GPA is important. Knowing what his GPA is needs to become a priority. Past experience says that kids who have a GPA over 3.0 usually know EXACTLY what it is. The reason is pretty simple: it is a thing of pride to have a 4.2 GPA.

Yes, it actually is possible to have a GPA over 4.0! Back in the caveman days when I went to school, 4.0 was the best you could have. (I do not know that from personal experience; I heard it somewhere.) Our players need to begin to see and experience the possibilities that go along with an improved GPA. As you can guess, I ask our kids about their GPAs regularly, and when I ask what their algebra grade is, the answer better not begin with, "I think…".

At Encina, we celebrate GPAs in many different ways. At our rallies, our kids introduce themselves to the student body by giving their name, their GPA, and then their position. I take the kids to a weekly Rotary meeting where they do the same thing.

The attitude on our campus is beginning to change. Our Athletic Director came into practice and observed our kids memorizing plays. He was impressed that our kids were called to the board and were teaching the other players. We call this metacognitive learning, and it carries over into other learning on campus.

When I talk with the kids about their GPA, I look at their Physical Education grade. It should be a given that they have an "A" in PE. I believe that PE is not much more than getting dressed to play for an hour, although a PE teacher would probably argue with me on that. If one of my student athletes has a "C" in PE, I am not a happy camper. Today, many kids think they are too cool for PE. They will not dress for it, and do not take it seriously. If one of my kids is not giving his best effort in PE, we will do some "extra PE" at 6:00 a.m. on Saturday morning.

As a coach, if I want a player to block better, I give him some drills to get the result I am looking for. The same thing applies in the classroom. We teach our players how to study. With our team, we teach creative memory skills to learn the plays. Then we show our Playmakers how they can use creative memory to learn history.

I just cringe when a mom tells me, "If his grades drop, he's off the team." I tell her, "I will teach him how to study. I'll make sure his grades and conduct are up, and I'll teach him important life skills that every young man should know. Then, IF his grades drop, he'll run until he understands why he should have good grades!" You see, we can be a team working together to get the job done.

ACTION POINT:

*Make sure your child is dressing for PE.
Check on missing assignments.
Get a note from the teacher saying there are no missing assignments.*

What Does Coach Have to Say About Girls?

I am a father of two girls, so you can imagine how I talk to the team. We coaches have some very candid conversations with our kids about how we need to treat girls. Last week, I ran one of our kids longer than he wanted because he suggested that one of the cheerleaders was a bit too heavy. I want the kids to understand that what boys say to girls, and how girls are treated by boys, leaves a lasting imprint on them.

Homecoming is an especially difficult time for girls. Homecoming involves a lot more than just trying to win a game. I have seen firsthand the anxiety girls feel over who gets "picked" to go to homecoming. We talk all week to the boys about the word "edify" and how it means to build someone up. We teach them the value and importance of making a girl feel good on campus. The girls are looking for acceptance. They want to be noticed. As a Playmaker, our kids will be taught how to be a young man of integrity. That means we will coach them on how to make homecoming a positive experience for a young lady.

One of the things we encourage our players to do is go to the girls' softball or soccer games. My daughter plays college soccer, so I have some appreciation of what kind of athletes these soccer players are, and how tough that game really is. I want our girls on campus to see that we support them. Our football team will show up and cheer for our girls in a respectful manner. We do it because it is the right thing to do.

Mrs. Roz is also treated well and given respect because we coach that. The players are taught to ask me how my wife is. That begins with me asking the player, "How's your mom doing? Tell her I asked about her."

Each day, we have opportunities to raise parents up. Single parents need this. Too often they get run over by sons who forget the huge job a parent has in being "the entire family" for her son. Your son's coach will help, if given the chance. Coaches today help fill that void. We need to model to these boys how to treat women every day. Together, we can and are making a difference.

ACTION POINT:

Talk about what it means when a girl says "No."

Let your mom wear your jersey. She has earned it.

Step Up and Be There!

I never allow a girlfriend to wear a game jersey on game day. To me that is sacrilegious. Mom wearing her son's jersey is a tradition that says mom is special. That honor is not meant for a girlfriend who may be gone by the end of the game. Mom, if you are at the game, you have earned that right, and then some. We need you at the game. This is the time to let your son know you support him unconditionally. This is your moment. Your having that jersey on means, "#62 belongs to me, and I am proud of him. I don't care if he sits the bench or is all-conference, #62 is MY SON!!"

I remember coming home after a game, and my mom was exhausted. I said something like, "Why are you tired? I played the game, not you." My mom taught me at a very early age that she played the game, too. She took each hit, and heard everything (good and bad) that was said about me in the stands.

My daughter plays college soccer. NOW I FINALLY UNDERSTAND what mom meant when she said she played the game, too. Your son may not understand this now, but it will come with time. When it comes to pain, moms have a hardwiring in them that dads just don't understand.

Senior Night is when the parents are honored for their son's participation in football. It is the happiest and saddest night of the season. My heart breaks for the kid who has no parents at the game to walk with him under the goal posts. Mrs. Roz, the other coaches, and I step in and walk with those kids. We are there because mom and dad are not.

Mom, step up and BE there! This is a special opportunity where you can create a memory. Mom, you MUST be there to get the rose and the picture that will be handed to you in front of the entire stadium. This is part of football, and your son wants you there. He may not be able to tell you that, but every kid wants his mom and dad there for Senior Night.

I teach the kids that they need to hug their mom more. Respecting moms should be a priority. Remember, Coach is in this game with you.

I give moms my cell number and tell them to call me whenever they need to. The kids hate it that mom has a direct line to me, and that's okay. I want my players to know that mom can get me on the phone for anything.

ACTION POINT:

Know the date of the last game.
Put the schedule on the fridge.

When to Let Go

My daughter, Katie, is my warrior poet. To me, that means she has the heart of a warrior. She plays the game like it is her last, and she truly loves it. That is the warrior in her. Katie is also my poet. She has a heart for the lost and forgotten and sees beauty in many things. Boys can be warrior poets, too.

Because Katie teaches me so much, I look for her lessons. I have watched how she handles her coaches without mommy and daddy coming to her rescue. Katie gets out of bed on her own, gets to practice on her own, and respects the game she plays like few I have seen.

Katie understands that her relationship with her coach is a priority, and she has experienced the good and the bad with that. Katie knows the difference between what it is to be the best high school player, and what it is like being a college player just trying to earn her spot on the field. She has experienced both. Her heart is an XXL (extra, extra large) but her body is an S (small). Katie inspires me. The last game she plays will not be a good day for "the ol' coach." She has given us so many joyful moments on and off the field. We have spent most of our weekends driving from one soccer game to another. There is no vacation that Mrs. Roz would choose over watching Katie play. You can have Maui. Our daughter plays the game, and we're going to be there for her.

Sports have kept Katie and me together during some tough growing up years. Like all families with teenagers, there are times when we think we have an alien in our house. Here is a shocker. I am a coach, yet Katie very rarely wants my opinion about soccer! As a dad, I am sure I am qualified, but she chooses to listen to the coach she plays for. Get it? Stay up in the stands and cheer loudly, but do not coach! That is what the guy on the sidelines is for. My daughter is teaching me that.

There are many times when I want to jump in and give my opinion about how her coach should be doing this or that, but my opinion does not count. The coach has that responsibility, not me. My daughter, by her actions, has taught me that many times. I love my warrior poet.

ACTION POINT:

Only talk to the coach after your child has.
Let your child work it out with coach.
Let coach know that you, as a parent, support him.

Treat Girls with Respect

I get a firsthand look at how boys see women from the conversations in the weight room and on the field. T-shirts are worn (not on my team) that are called "wife beaters." Songs are played (not by my team) telling about how women are abused in our culture. Part of my job is to create a model for how a functional couple navigates through life. That is one of the reasons the kids come to my house. I want them to see us interact. As coaches, we show our kids, in the best way we can, how precious women are to us, and how they are to be treated.

A Playmakers coach can help by providing rules for dating. One of the things we tell our kids is, "Treat your date like she was Coach's daughter." We go a step further. I make it a point to meet the player's girlfriend. I let it be known that if she is not treated well, to just let Coach know. We do it in a fun manner, but I want the message to be clear: you will run a deep trench into the track if you mistreat a girl.

As I've already mentioned, we teach the boys to treat their date with respect. In a perfect world, that is dad's job. It is so special when these lessons are taught by the man whose job it is in the first place! We dads (almost 40 percent) have bailed out. We have left that job to someone else, or we have convinced ourselves that we can do it on weekends, or as a single parent. As a Playmakers coach, we have to sub and fill in so the job gets done. There is so much work to be done to teach these boys about being a real man and what true masculinity is all about. Until the dads come home with a plan, we will do the best we can.

Because sex gets confused with masculinity, we teach our players that there is no badge of honor with this issue. I often say, "What you do with that girl will be a memory for her for a lifetime." I am not stupid here, but I know that when a coach says this, it may be the FIRST time the kids have heard this from an adult they respect. A good coach cannot let these kids try to figure this out on their own! We must coach it now.

ACTION POINT:

Let your child know what your dating rules are.

His Heart Is Not Too Small

Let me tell you about my 100-Pound Club. The 100-Pound Club is for the kids who begin playing high school football weighing less than 100 pounds. The club is growing, and these kids are great fun. The "Terminator" and Bobby "Kicker" Malloy are just a couple of them. These are kids whose parents have told me they thought their sons were joking when they came home and said, "Dad, I am trying out for the football team."

These kids not only gain confidence, they earn the respect of the entire campus because of our policy that EVERY kid plays every game. One of the most enjoyable parts of coaching football is watching these kids as they grow, change, and develop.

Football prepares your son for so many things in life. You MUST allow him the opportunity to become a warrior poet. It is for him to decide this, not mom. This is a rite into true masculinity, and you cannot hold that back.

From time to time we hear about a football player having a serious permanent injury. As with any sport, that can happen, but these incidents are few and far between. As a mom, you need to know what the risks and benefits of this sport are. Find someone who is qualified who can answer your questions so "Johnny" can play this wonderful sport without your losing sleep over it. Remember: your son's football coach is guiding your son into manhood. Talk with his coach when you need to and be proud of the fact that "Johnny" is learning how to play this great game.

ACTION POINT:

Let him play.

Fill Them Up!

My dad is one of my heroes, and yet, all my adult life, I have chased my tail seeking his approval. Finally, when I became 51, he gave me his blessing. I am 52 years old now, and I cry like a baby thinking about how my dad is proud of me.

I teach kids to ask their parents, "Are you proud of me?" because moms and dads don't say that to their kids very often. Most parents need coaching in this area, and some are working from an outdated playbook. This needs to change. Parents need to be coached on what boys need to hear so they can become the masculine men they are meant to be.

Our kids thrive on approval. I have had Bloods and Crips get tears in their eyes when I look them in the eye and tell them, "Son, I am proud of you." Our kids crave that. They just don't want to let us know because they want to look cool. There is nothing in the world like looking your team in the eye and seeing each one of their faces when you tell them you are proud of them.

We need to encourage our kids like we are coaching Little League. They need to hear positive affirmation at every opportunity. They will respond to it over time, and it will become infectious. My daughter hears it regularly, and she will continue to hear it as long as I can get it out of my mouth. "I am proud of you" comes out of my mouth almost every day to one of my kids, at home and at school. These affirmations are food for their soul, and they need plenty of them. Affirmations are part of the Playmakers coaching playbook. We teach coaches that you can only holler at a kid when you're happy.* We also teach our coaches to be clear about what they want. Tell the kids what you DO want, not what you don't want.

Here is how we are passing this down to our Playmakers. We tell them the seniors are "the dads of the team," which means they have responsibilities to the freshmen. This includes having the seniors tell the freshmen they are proud of them. Where else can you site examples where kids learn to say "I am proud of you" to other kids? This is just another example of how football teaches life lessons, so don't tell me your son is "too small" to learn that!

Remember, we are in this together. One of the many things that I am proud of is how we are teaching kids to give each other positive affirmations and to say, "I love you." We are teaching youths to mentor youths. This is being taught by committed Playmakers coaches who will do what it takes to get the job done.

*My deep thanks to Tree Plumbtree for this great bit of wisdom.

ACTION POINT:

*Tell them you are proud of them and why.
Tell them that they "are good enough."*

Rainy Sunday, watching a game with Pop: PERFECT DAY.

I Owe Pop Everything

As I said earlier, my dad is my hero, and we don't have much time left. He has given me a "game plan" on how to be a man. Not a perfect one, but one that gives me some skills that make being a father easier. He has taught me so many things. We have fun doing very simple things. His health does not allow him to do much, but what we do together is golden.

Pop is a warrior who gives more to kids now than ever before. He loves it when we bring "the family" to his home so he can meet them. He has a presence with them, and they show him such respect. These kids have taught him a lot as well.

You can't believe how much fun it is for the two of us to cook breakfast together. We get in the kitchen and make a mess, and sometimes bacon and eggs come out, too. Pretty macho, huh? Two big old Germans in the kitchen like two grandmas arguing over whose biscuits are better. It was Pop who taught me that it is okay for a dad to cook breakfast on Sunday. That's just one of my many lessons from Pop.

Not every kid gets that experience with their dad, but many of my players have stood by the stove with me cooking eggs or pancakes for Mrs. Roz and Katie. I teach the kids how to flip eggs, and that is quite a sight. We have had to sacrifice a few eggs to learn that. We have begun making more omelets until we get the egg flip down better.

I might not ever play cribbage after Pop is gone as there is no one who cheats like him. He is a master at cheating and winning. We argue at the table, and the entire house has to endure Pop and me competing. After that ritual, we settle in the living room and watch a game. We don't care who is playing. It is just Pop and me and a few invited (and ignored) guests or family watching the game that has kept us bonded through the years. What makes it even more perfect? It begins to rain, and we take a nap.

My prayer for your son is that he and his dad (or another father-figure) can become best friends. It may not be now, and it may take a lifetime, but the wait is worth it. Until then, your young man can watch the game at my house.

ACTION POINT:

Teach your kid to cook something.
Watch a game with him.

Healing Their Wounds

I have spent a lot of hours with men who have carried the scars of what their dads did and didn't do. The stories are endless and too complicated to include here, but I know that too many men love their sons and do not know how to express it because of their own brokenness.

Here is where a Playmakers coach comes in. When we can get a boy to talk about the hurt or disappointment he is feeling, we are making progress. As a coach, hearing the boy's frustration is heartbreaking, yet we can offer some understanding and a game plan for redemption now or in the future.

Mom, I realize that this gets complicated, and one size does not fit all. The point is, in MOST cases, a son needs HIS father. Mom, let me coach you here. This is NOT about YOU. It is about your son and his needs. You cannot be dad, and sometimes Coach can help you with your son.

We men who did not have a dad in the picture have scars that get passed along. Too many times I hear men say they never heard the encouraging words they needed to hear from their dad. I do not want to counsel here, but rather get the job done. The focus is your son. He needs to hear a man he respects say, "I love you." We coaches say it regularly. I want our kids to hear a man say it unashamedly. I want them to hear me say to Coach Lambdin (our linebacker coach), "Coach, I love you." Playmakers are taught to love each other.

Mom, this stuff may not be easy to read. I know your scars can be deep, too. Remember, though, we are in this together. As I tell my team, if it was easy, everyone would play football. So as the head coach, let me say, "I need you in the drill." Allow us to help. This means that you may have to allow a relationship to develop between your son and his father, even though it hurts you, but as I tell our players sometimes, this is NOT about you. Let's focus on getting the ball in the end zone. That means having your son hear "I love you" from a man with whom he can develop a quality relationship.

> ## *ACTION POINT:*
>
> *Say "I love you" more.*
> *Remember, he needs a man*
> *who can be trusted.*

You Are Being Sent

When our kids graduate, I tell them, "You are not leaving, you are being sent."* I want them to know that they have been coached to go make a difference in the community. I want them to know Coach expects that. They have been coached, and they know the play; now it is time for them to go get it done. You see, they are Playmakers for life. They need to know they can always count on Coach, and we have their backs. They are part of "the family," and that is the kind of family I want them to create. They know that Coach will ALWAYS be there, and they need to ALWAYS be there for their family.

I just got an e-mail from Jason Martz, one of our graduates. Jason is a hero. He just sent me pictures about his latest promotion. He is now an Enlisted Surface Warfare Specialist onboard the *USS Gridley*. I just love typing that. Even though he lost his father during high school, he graduated with a 4.0 GPA. He could have gone down the wrong road. There were times when he was close, but he had too much character. He is a Playmaker. He defends our country and, as soon as he gets home, he calls me, and we have dinner. Then he comes and speaks to the younger Playmakers. He is a hero we can be proud of.

I don't know how many times we told Jason that we love him and we are proud of him; probably too many to count. He only played quarterback his senior year. He took over the job when our starter could not play. From the moment he took over, you could see that Jason was a leader and would give you everything he had. He has character, which means doing the right thing when no one is looking. That is one of the characteristics of a hero. Anyone who knows me knows that no one is good enough to date my daughter (let alone marry her), but Jason wouldn't get thrown out of the house.

Jason is a kid who can be counted on. That quality is built into him. I wish I could take credit for it, but it is in his hardwiring. All Jason needed was a coach who fire-hosed him with praise and attention. A bond was created between us that will last for a lifetime. I can never replace the loss of his dad, which today he still cannot talk about. When he IS ready, I will be there, and we will go spend all the time he needs.

*I am deeply grateful to Joe Ehrmann, who shared this concept with me over breakfast several years ago.

> ### **ACTION POINT:**
> *Talk about graduation and how proud you will be.*

Hummer and Other Heroes

"9-11" is part of our history. Most of my Playmakers were about eight years old, and some remember it. Like you, I know exactly where I was when I heard the Tower went down. It is our history. As a coach, I have used it for many teaching opportunities. The first question I ask the kids is, "How many airplanes went down on 9-11?" I get the answer of "3" as many times as I get the answer of "4." Some of us forget flight 93 in which a true hero, Todd Beamer, led the charge by keeping our Nation's Capitol safe.

Todd Beamer formed a team, created a plan, and executed a play beyond our comprehension. He must have known what his destiny was when he got a group of men (his team) together and led them on a mission to destiny. He organized his team and rallied their support to overtake the plane. His goal was to save lives and not be a victim. The cockpit was his end zone. They had one play to get it done. I know that I do not have that kind of courage and resolve, but Todd did. Todd Beamer is a man who I am honored just to write about. I aspire to meet his family some day and just say, "Thank you." Todd

Beamer is a man with a story that we need to keep alive. As Coach, I use his courageous story to inspire future heroes who will make a difference when their opportunity comes.

David Humm is another hero of mine. Hummer will be mad at me for mentioning him on the same page with Todd Beamer. He will get over it. Hummer took me under his wing when we were in training camp with the Raiders and made an impression on me that has lasted for 30 years. It makes me proud to call him my friend. I love David Humm, and I know he loves me, too. I talk about Hummer regularly at practice and at most of my speaking presentations. He models living with character and integrity every day of his life. He gives of himself like few I have ever met. To know why he is a hero, you will have to do a little work and go find an article called "BUT LIFE IS GOOD...," by Donna Miesbach. It's in the Archives on the Gleanings page of her web site, www.donnamiesbach.com.

We need real heroes now more than ever. We need men we can point to and say, "That is what a real hero looks like." They are not on MTV, and very few of them are on ESPN. They are not who we see at the movies or in a video game. They are riding in the back of an airplane, and at home doing ordinary things. They are fathers who will stay home, raise their families, and finish the job.

I am looking for Playmakers who will come and speak to us when they "go pro," players who I will not have to pay a speaker's fee to, or talk to their agent or posse. I just need a hero like David Humm who will say, "Where do you need me, Coach? I am a Playmaker, and I am here."

ACTION POINT:

*Ask your son who his heroes are, and why.
Tell him who your heroes are.*

Laugh and Cry Every Day

I am the biggest baby you will ever meet. I always cry at our End of the Year Banquet. One summer when we were up at Tahoe, I looked at one of my players, a young man by the name of Luis Martinez, and I just lost it right there in front of two hundred people. Luis was telling us about losing his brother and how he is playing for him now.

Tears are not uncommon for me. I come from a family who cries a lot. We love each other, and that means we show it with tears and laughter.

I have been in conversation with man after man who says he never saw his dad cry. Who made that rule, and how is it working? I show our kids all my emotions so they can see who I really am. I want them to know it is okay to hurt and show it. We men have been sold the wrong plan that says we cannot ever show when we are hurt. This feeds into false masculinity and image management issues that we MUST break through. Too often football feeds into this concept. Players are taught not to show pain, and never let them see you hurt. That sends a mixed message to our kids, one that boys carry into manhood.

The question here is, how many men have been watered down to too few laughs and cries? So many think they need to have their "poker face" on so people cannot see beyond their armor. I just want to meet the man who that really works for. That man cannot tell me he understands that true masculinity means having deep quality relationships and being involved in a cause larger than himself.* Playmakers aspires to break that cycle.

In my mind's eye, I can see this great reunion in thirty years with all of our Playmakers in a huge room, and I'll ask, "How many of you are married and not divorced?" With all my heart, I pray that more than 50 percent of the hands go up. I hope that we are a group of men who committed to go the distance and did not bail out. I hope Playmakers had something to do with that. At that reunion, if the tears are flowing and the laughs are loud, I'll know we did our job.

*This is a spin on another one of Joe Ehrmann's great pieces of wisdom. Thanks, Joe!

ACTION POINT:

Let him know that it is good to cry. Ask him what makes him cry for a good reason.

Way Beyond the Game

One of the finest guys I know is my buddy from college, Rick Garretson. Rick mentors me now in coaching football and is one of the coaches I turn to for guidance on many occasions. I was privileged to be at his dad's funeral and celebrate the life and career of Darell Garretson. Saying goodbye to one of the NBA's greatest officials was both a happy and sad occasion. As good as he was at officiating, Darell was an even better man.

Darell was a nationally known man of celebrity status. The funeral looked like a Who's Who of professional basketball. Darell was honored at a wonderful celebration of over three hundred people. What amazed me was who was asked to speak at the funeral. It was my buddy, Larry Toner, Rick's high school football coach. Rick's Coach assisted and counseled my friend through the tough loss of his dad. When a man who has played the game of football is in crisis, he can usually turn to his coach who will respond like a Playmaker and get the job done.

We teach our team that we are a family, and we say that a lot. You will often hear, "We are like a family around here." Understand, we ARE a family, and that means we are learning about accountability and character together. Each day, our kids see one of our coaches (the dads of the family) make decisions that affect the entire family. These are decisions that the kids can resource later in life. They usually know what decision Coach would make about issues of character.

We want the kids to know they can count on us now and in the future. It begins with them coming to us for things like a reference for a summer job or their first credit application. We let them know they can count on us for advice on anything from college assistance to funeral arrangements. This is the best part of being a Playmakers coach. I have had calls where kids need to know what to do when their Mom goes to jail. They need to know how to get groceries when mom and dad are not around. These are just some of the ways we help keep kids on track and make it possible for them to endure the challenges they face with little to no means.

ACTION POINT:

Ask your son who his favorite coach is.
Ask him why he is his favorite.

Look Me in the Eye and Tell Me What Happened

Part of being "old school" means that we teach respect and discipline. We begin by teaching kids how to shake hands and introduce themselves to an adult. We teach the "traditional handshake," as it is still the accepted one, whether you're at an interview or meeting your girlfriend's father. It does not surprise me that kids today do not know how to introduce themselves to an adult. If one of them wins the Heisman Trophy, I want them to know how to shake hands and introduce themselves.

I also have a policy of no do-rags, no skull caps, and no earrings. I want to know the kids without the false props they have. Frankly, I want to know if their hats are more important than being part of our family. This policy helps bring us together right away, as we all look the same and are not caught up in things that are not important. If kids are more interested in an earring than learning what our rules are, I want to know that at the beginning. That gives me a starting point with that young man.

Sometimes, when disagreements happen, a player will want to come and talk to me. I welcome that. There are rules in talking to a coach. Here is the first one: only one of us is going to talk at a time. The kids need to learn that during a conversation, one talks and one listens. (It is a pretty good rule at home, too.) Again, we are teaching these kids how to communicate when they are in college, or working on a job, or talking to their significant other. They learn these skills on the football field from coaches who demand it. Then, over time, they begin to communicate at home in the same way.

Mom, here is where we can work together. Let's say you are having a disagreement with your son about what time you want him home. He is arguing his case loudly, and you can't get a word in. That is the time for you to say to him, "Is this how you talk to Coach? I am going to call him right now so I can hear how you'd talk to him about this." That usually will settle things down enough for you to get your point across.

We can partner together and teach these kids lessons that they must know when they become adults. Today I see kids who just have no clue what acceptable communication is. They have seen yelling and how the biggest person "wins" the argument by being the loudest. Not Playmakers. We show respect, and communicate in a character-based manner. If we can (and we do) get kids to say, "Yes, Coach!" or "Yes, Sir!"—and they do it with no earring or skull cap—we are teaching them life skills and giving them tools that will empower them for a lifetime.

ACTION POINT:

*Get the coach's cell phone number.
Let your son know that you
have it in your phone.
Call coach in front of your son
so he knows that you will.*

I Care About Your Character

Shaping kids can be challenging. There are times when we disagree, particularly when the rules are character-based. There are times when the shortcut seems like the road to take. My kids know I will cloud up and rain on them when I need to. Because we have a relationship, time and time again they will hear from me, "Am I doing this because I don't like you or because I care about you?" They know I care. Then we go run until I am sure I have gotten my point across.

I have benched kids who are grade eligible just because they are not giving their best effort. That hurts, because in most of our games, we need every kid. I have asked kids to apologize to their teammates for not holding up their end. Kids need to learn to apologize, and I am not sure where else that is being taught.

Here is a tool I hope you find helpful. Sit down and discuss with your son how Coach talks to him and the other players on the team. Ask him how we solve problems in the football family. Ask him what the consequences are for being late, or embarrassing the family. Your son can tell you exactly how we would handle it.

You have the same ability to establish rules in your home. If you need help, use the same rules we have in the football family. We are here to help you with the huge task you have in helping that boy become a young man of character.

I have learned that most kids will rise to the bar that you set for them. The question is, have you set the bar? Our players check in regularly with their coach, so I do not understand why they would not call and check in with you as their parent.

Saying to your son, "If you don't (whatever), I will pull you off the team," does not work. It just creates a bigger wedge between you and your son. Instead, try this: "If you don't do (whatever), I will call Coach and we'll let him handle it." That is music to my ears because you make ME the bad guy, and now we are working together on the problem. When I hear a parent tell me, "He can play football as long as his grades are good or his conduct is good," my response is, "Have him choose another sport because I want kids who are going to stay, not bail out." If they learn that they can bail out now, they will bail out later.

ACTION POINT:

Make a commitment that your son will not be removed from the team. Only "holler" when you're happy.

Hold Them Accountable. We Do.

Mom, we have rules. There should be rules in your home as well. Our kids do not need to be out running the streets after hours. Nothing good happens after 11:00 p.m. Your son needs to understand that if he is part of the football family, he will honor your rules. If you do not have a rule about curfew, make one. Your child needs boundaries. Again, make me the bad guy. Make me the person who creates football consequences if he does not comply.

Perhaps you do not know the rules of accountability that we have established and that he is already playing to, but you can ask your son, "What time do you think coach wants you in?" That can cut through it pretty quickly. Your son has been coached. He knows the right answer. I have leverage because he wants to play football, so we can work together and get the result you are looking for. I have curfew, and I have rules. You can use mine, if yours are not working. Let us help you. The fact that your son is part of the football family makes him accountable to all of us.

Now let me turn the table here for a minute. If you and I are a team and we are on the coaching staff together, think of yourself as the position coach for your son. We have established rules for curfew, grade performance, accountability, and conduct. That makes us all a better team. The point is, you must coach your position. You now have some leverage with your player (son) if you know what is expected and are willing to hold your player accountable. When a player gets out of line, usually that kid is sent to the Head Coach who makes the disciplinary corrections. You can do the same thing if what you are doing now is not working well.

Football coaches do what works well. We are creatures of habit. Parents need to do the same. If you find something that is working, continue to do it. If your track record is not working, and you continue to use the same plan, you cannot expect a different result. Run a new play, or coach the kid in a different manner. If you are not sure what to do, that is okay. We attend coaching clinics every year to figure out what to do. If you sit down with your son's coach and develop a relationship with him, you both will get it handled.

ACTION POINT:

Set a curfew with agreed upon consequences.
Let your child know that coach knows what that curfew time is.

Love Them Harder

Our kids need to do more talking, because relationships—not playing XBox—build their character so they can be successful young men. I see firsthand how difficult it is for kids who are trying to fix their parents' marriage while dealing with teen issues and peer pressure. It just is not easy for our kids today. I have kids who are working a part time job, not for their first car, but to help with rent. How can that be expected of a sixteen-year-old? If we can just provide a healthy outlet for them and a place where they can feel safe, literally, we are doing our job.

We teach "family." We believe that is a good thing. I had a kid say he did not want to be part of the "family" because all his hurts revolved around his family. At least we have him talking about it and beginning to open up a bit. If we don't change his reality of "family," what chance does he have of being a functioning husband or father? I love this kid. He has spent several nights at my home so he can just sleep and eat. He has literally been homeless for most of his teen years.

I hope people of affluence read what I just wrote. People in the suburbs might not have an up-close understanding that we have kids who are homeless, sleeping in cars, and living in weekly motels regularly. These kids did not ask for the hand they have been dealt. They are living with the choices their moms and dads have made. For more information on how you can make a difference for these kids, contact me. I will be happy to talk to you.

We also teach these kids that they must contribute to our community. We teach them that they have the power to do things to help themselves. Any kid can wash a car and earn $10. They can serve in the community. That is one of the pillars of being a Playmaker.

So what do my coaching staff and I do? We create situations where kids will talk. We do it over the stove cooking. We do it in Coach's back yard pulling weeds. We do it at our Tahoe retreats. We do it while driving home, or at 6:00 a.m. when they are running because they were late. Every day we are trying to change the direction of a lost or forgotten group of kids.

ACTION POINT:

Start conversations with questions that begin with:
What do you think…?
Give me your opinion…
Help me understand…

You Can Play Through It

When a kid calls me and tells me he can't come to practice (when he never misses a game with a cold), I am not a happy camper. I will tell him to get to practice in the same manner that we go to work with a cold. I know there are times when someone is too sick to be there, but those are few and far between. Play through it, and learn the lesson of being dependable when you don't feel well. It will help you later in life.

Going to the family doctor can be a recipe for disaster for a football coach. The family doctor will tell you to take two weeks off for a broken toenail. Usually he or she did not play football, so the answer is always, "Take a week off, and don't aggravate it." We need kids who will play through minor injuries. I always ask a kid who does not think he can practice: "If this was game day, would you be playing?"

This may seem pretty macho to you, but that is not the purpose of practicing with a headache. Once they are working and providing for their family, we want them to know they can perform under tough circumstances. Where else is this lesson being taught? Where else do they learn about performing and getting the job done because someone else is depending on them? When Playmakers put others first in the football family, they learn this value.

I know you are the parent, and ultimately it is your call when your child practices and when he doesn't. All I am saying is, let's work on this together. I have a clear rule that we live by. If you miss practice, you will not play, even at the risk of the team losing the game. We will win our share of games with the kids who are there every day, learning the character skills of dependability and placing others above self.

> ## *ACTION POINT:*
>
> *Do not miss an entire day for a dentist appointment. Let the coach or trainer determine if he should sit out. You can still go to practice and learn without participating in practice.*

"I'll Try" Won't Get It Done

My daughter, Katie, is a great young woman. I love to hear her tell stories about things she remembers from her growing years. When she tells her stories, she uses what she calls her "dad-isms." Katie tells me I have "the look," and it goes right through her. I know she practices "the look" so she can have it down when she becomes a mother.

It really bothers Katie when she has trouble making the right decision. Like most kids, Katie KNOWS the right decision. Sometimes it's just hard to follow through on it, so when she needs help with making the RIGHT choice, I will ask her, "What do you think your soccer coach would say?"

You see, most decisions are simple. Yes, they are simple. It is not hard to know what the right decision is. That part is easy. The hard part is ACTING ON the right decision. I tell our Playmakers, "The decision is simple, not easy." All of the teachings in the book that I try to live my life by are simple, but they are not easy.

Our kids hear me say often, "Do not tell me you will try. Tell me you will be there. Pick a road: yes or no, and make a decision." You cannot have it both ways. I want my kids to know that. That is what I'm teaching them.

Today too many of our kids say things like "I'll try," "I'm not sure," and "Maybe." They can make a decision on XBox much easier than on character-based issues. I need kids who can pick a road quickly and move fast in the right direction. Football is just the dress rehearsal for that character trait. That's why, when they're working through decisions they think are life altering, like do I go to senior cut day (my daughter will love that one), I tell the kids, "Make a decision and pick a road. Yes or no."

ACTION POINT:

Tell your child "Yes" or "No," not "I'll try."
Compliment them for a good answer.
Tell them they are becoming
someone who can be depended on.

Let's Be Decisive

Coaches often tell their players, "Go hit somebody," so let me be clear here. "Hit somebody" means on the field, not in the classroom, or on the street. Every kid and every coach knows that means don't make excuses! I just need a yes or no answer, particularly on the football field when we have to communicate quickly. So when my kids (and adults) want to ramble on and on about their story, I tell them to get to the point.

Today, as when I was a kid, we try to talk our way through situations when what we really need to do is just face the issue, stand in integrity, and come clean. This is where most learning occurs. It is also where we can make progress. I don't want to hear, "The dog ate my homework." I want our kids to learn the value of acting with integrity and moving on from there.

As it relates to the football field specifically, it doesn't matter if you have your pro-style gloves or your name on the back of your jersey. Those things are nice, but they are not what this most beautiful game is about. I have kids who do not have their own cleats or a bag to carry their gear in. We need players on the field who care about the game, not just themselves.

When we are on the field and in the classroom, we need to be decisive men and women of character. Certainly we coaches need to have a compassionate ear and heart to help mold these kids. But there are also times when we just need for a kid to not worry about the small, insignificant things and JUST DO IT.

> ## *ACTION POINT:*
>
> *Tell your kid to quit complaining and just do it!*

It's All About Character

Our After-School Program with elementary school kids has taught us so much. We are watching these young kids learn and demonstrate character daily. They will memorize, repeat, and eventually put into practice the character lessons being taught. They practice these teachings in the classroom as well as on the field.

Character is the foundation for all we hope to achieve with Playmakers. If everything we do is run through that filter, we believe that our kids will have a track to run on, both now and later in life. As you look at the societal challenges of today, we see character breakdowns time and time again. When we see acts of heroism from common ordinary people, it's usually character rising to the top.

Playmakers aspires to leave a legacy as an organization or team that builds people of character. We believe that we, as a society, are desperately in need of people of character. Character produces servant leadership.

Leaders make people around them better people. The more people embrace character and leadership as a way of life, the more we will see an exciting and inspiring generation of leaders rise up and become the citizens they are capable of being.

In Conclusion

Parents, I do not intend to convince you that some quotes and a brief explanation will be the solution to all the challenges you face in raising your child. What I do hope to do is offer a new and possibly untapped resource that may provide you some relief or assistance. Until the men come home and finish the job of helping raise the kids they produced, we coaches are just providing a band aid to the problem. That is a beginning, though, and we will continue to try to provide more help to you.

As coaches, we are creating young men who are learning to care for something besides themselves. We are creating servants and leaders. We are coaching coaches to do a better job with your kids, and to help fill the void left by broken marriages and unprepared parents. We have taken over a team of broken homes that is way behind in the game. The divorce rate is hovering at 40 percent, and nearly four out of every ten of our kids live in a home without their biological father. Coaches can assist with this massive challenge. We can make this a winning team.

Playmakers is growing a stronger team of men, women, and corporate players who are catching the vision of loving lost kids and creating men who will finish the game. We are offering more clinics and resources to kids, as well as coaches. Our website includes a blog that allows us to communicate with you and your child easier. We have begun to partner with law enforcement agencies to show Playmakers families the positive side of law enforcement. As we grow and learn together, and determine that this is a game we WILL NOT LOSE, we will begin to change a kid, a family and a community.

Coach Roz

Partnering with Playmakers

Playmakers is an organization of coaches, teachers, mentors, and everyday people like you and me who genuinely care about the welfare of today's young people. We work together, each in our own way, to help children become responsible citizens of tomorrow. While our outreach embraces all children, our focus is especially on disadvantaged, at-risk children—kids who have had a tough beginning in life and who are in need of guidance, support, and encouragement. As Playmakers, we strive to give these kids a game plan to follow so they can reach beyond their present circumstances and realize their dreams.

Playmakers is run entirely through the financial partnership of its supporters. Because of the generosity of people who care, we are able to maintain our After-School Reading/Mentoring Program and our Coaching Clinics and Camps without charge to our participants. These partnerships include Rotary, Optimists, Vision Service Plan, Chicago Fire, and many more. Donations are always gratefully accepted.

The Playmakers program began in the Sacramento area. From there it spread throughout California, and is now reaching not only a national, but also an international, audience. There are many ways to be part of this rapidly-growing program.

If you'd like to volunteer in some capacity, or contribute whatever special talent you have in your own unique way, please know we would welcome it. Just let us know what you have in mind, and we'll find a way to plug you in.

The Playmakers philosophy can be applied in a variety of settings, including music and the arts. If that is your forte, let us know. We'd be happy to help you get the Playmakers program up and running.

The Playmakers organization is made up of many hands, many hearts, and many willing feet. We invite you to be among us.

Coach Greg Roeszler ~ 916-220-1284
E-mail: coachroz@theplaymakers.org
Web site: www.theplaymakers.org
Blog: www.theplaymakers.org/blog

Invite Coach Roz to Speak to Your Group

Coach Roz welcomes the opportunity to speak to groups anywhere, any time. His dynamic, heartfelt presentations have a way of enabling his listeners to see possibilities they have not previously considered, and helping them find the means within themselves to reach a little higher and be a little stronger.

Coach Roz speaks on a variety of subjects at corporate functions, before both civic and faith-based groups, as well as youth leadership seminars and churches. His talks to sales and business management teams open new horizons for his listeners, making it easier for them to "think outside the box."

Coach Roz has also had great success speaking at group homes. His presentations are laced with humor and underscored with compassion and sensitivity to the needs of his listeners, whether they are staff or residents.

Roz has a special gift of being able to reach the hearts of even the most troubled children, leaving them with a feeling of validation and worth they may not have felt before. His ability to communicate with even the most withdrawn of children is remarkable, just as is his ability to bring hope and possibility to adults in group homes and rehabilitation centers. In addition, Roz is able to give the staff at these centers a fresh perspective, both on their work and on their life.

When you invite Coach Roz to speak to your organization, he becomes part of your team, and you of his. To bring Coach Roz to your group, or your area, he can be reached through any of the methods below:

Coach Greg Roeszler ~ 916-220-1284
E-mail: coachroz@theplaymakers.org
Web site: www.theplaymakers.org
Blog: www.theplaymakers.org/blog

Coaching for Character Clinics

All across the country, our cities are filled with fatherless children. The residual effects of our fatherless society are beyond comprehension, yet there is hope. Coach Roz is calling on our coaches to stand up and teach our children to be real heroes by becoming men and women who can be counted on. Roz's clinics give coaches a road map for building character that they can use with the kids back home. Roz shows them how to make life safer for children. He teaches coaches how to be there for the long haul, so they can set an example the kids will not forget.

In addition to coaching techniques, these one-day clinics show coaches how to communicate with kids and other coaches in an effective and positive manner. The purpose of these clinics is to show people how to coach for the larger purpose of building a life, and not "just" to have a winning football team. Character-based leadership, responsible citizenship, and team building are just a few of the topics that are covered. These clinics bring coaches, team captains and team leaders together where they can share their concerns, ask their questions, and then work together toward their common goal.

Through these clinics, Coach Roz and his staff are developing an ever-broadening network of support for coaches and for the underprivileged kids they work with. Volunteer coaches from both high school and college levels assist in running the clinics and camps.

Each summer, Roz's Clinic for Parents offers specific tools that help moms and dads guide their children through the difficult growing years.

Playmakers also serves as a Coach's Certification Center, providing the hours needed for Youth Coaching Certification.

All of our clinics are funded by private donations and corporate sponsorships. If you would like to bring a Coaching Clinic to your area, or if you would like to learn more about this unique way of coaching, contact Coach Roz.

Coach Greg Roeszler ~ 916-220-1284
E-mail: coachroz@theplaymakers.org
Web site: www.theplaymakers.org
Blog: www.theplaymakers.org/blog

Playmakers' Free Summer Sports Camps

Coach Roz and his dedicated team of assistants run free summer camps for football and other sports in CA for children from ages seven through high school. With enough advance notice, he will hold camps anywhere else in the country. The camps are coordinated with local coaches, as well as with coaches who travel from other states to help with this outreach. At these camps, children not only have a chance to learn important skills in football, they are also coached on what "real" character is, and what it means to be a responsible member of your family and your community. In other words, Playmakers is training the next generation of leaders by teaching young student athletes about themselves, their potential, and how to serve others.

In exchange for the free camp, the children are expected to maintain good grades in school. They are also required to perform community service as a group, under the guidance of the coaches. The results have been startling. Kids who before were fighting simply because they were born on different streets have learned that they all have the same hopes and dreams, and even more, that they can become friends.

Coach Roz also holds youth quarterback camps where young quarterbacks can learn specialized skills and receive leadership training.

If you'd like to have a Playmakers camp in your area, we would need for a local person to organize pre-camp activities, find volunteers, and connect Coach Roz with leaders in your community. Having a "point" person is key to our being able to come to a new area.

Volunteers are a necessary component at our camps. We need people to help with registration and check in. We need people to set up the field and man the water station. We always need a First Aid person and a trainer. We need a liaison who can link our efforts with the local law enforcement and the Fire Department. People can also donate food and other supplies and make donations to help with the ongoing cost of these camps.

Together, we are making a difference. The world of tomorrow is in our children's hands. What better way to assure them a promising future than to teach them skills that will empower them for a lifetime!

If you'd like to bring a Free Playmakers Summer Sports Camp to your area, contact Coach Roz. He would welcome your call.

Coach Greg Roeszler ~ 916-220-1284
E-mail: coachroz@theplaymakers.org
Web site: www.theplaymakers.org
Blog: www.theplaymakers.org/blog

About Playmakers' Books

Greg "Coach Roz" Roeszler has dedicated his life to helping underprivileged, at-risk children, wherever they are. These books were born out of that passion. Written with wisdom, humor, and deep compassion, each book is certain to touch the heart of its readers. The concepts contained within these books apply to every aspect of life, not just the game of football. The books not only speak directly to their targeted audience, they offer deep insight to a general audience as well.

Coach Roz works closely with single parents of his students, many of whom are in need of guidance and encouragement. Roz makes a point of forming a team with them not only to help them, but also to ultimately help their child as well. Over time, Roz developed a repertoire of sayings that he used with his parents. It was a natural extension for him to collect those sayings and put them into a book so they could be used as a reference. Thus, *Coaching Character and Leadership: A Playbook for Parents*, was born.

Many of the children Roz works with come from extremely difficult circumstances. Some are homeless, parentless, or fatherless. Their story needs to be told, and solutions must be provided. Roz believes that at least some of the answers can be found within the kids themselves. Through the game of football, Roz teaches the kids to be accountable to each other, and to care about each other by being part of the football family. Slowly the kids have learned what it means to be a responsible citizen of their community, to help and serve others, and to reach beyond themselves simply because it is the right thing to do.

After seeing the difference this approach made with his own students, Coach Roz began working with coaches all over the State of California, teaching them how to coach character while coaching football. As his clinics increased in number, so did the need for his first manual on coaching for character. In his own unique way, Coach Roz shows his readers how to focus on the deeper values that lie hidden within the game. It is Roz's belief that when taught correctly, the game of football can be a blueprint for life. *Coaching for a Bigger Win: A Playbook for Coaches*, contains that blueprint, at least in part.

These books, written out of the abundance of Roz's heart, come from a man who has been able to connect with a larger vision for his life. It is his hope, and his prayer, that those who read these books will be guided to find a larger vision for their own life as well.

Order Form

Coaching Character and Leadership: A Playbook for Parents

Price: $12.95 x _____ (number of copies) $ _____

Case: $300 x _____ (number of cases) 24 books per case $ _____

Sales Tax (7% when shipped to Nebraska addresses only) $ _____

Shipping & Handling: $5 per book, $25 per case   Total $ _____

Coaching for a Bigger Win: A Playbook for Coaches

Price: $12.95 x _____ (number of copies) $ _____

Case: $300 x _____ (number of cases) 24 books per case $ _____

Sales Tax (7% when shipped to Nebraska addresses only) $ _____

Shipping & Handling: $5 per book, $25 per case   Total $ _____

Customer Name: _____

Shipping Address: _____

City: _____ State: _____ Zip: _____

Telephone: (____) _____

Email: _____

Payment Method:

☐ Visa   ☐ Master Card   ☐ American Express   ☐ Discover

Name on Card: _____

Billing Address (if different from above): _____

City: _____ State: _____ Zip: _____

Card Number: _____ CVV: _____

Total Amount to be Charged: _____

Signature: _____ Exp. Date: _____

Mail This Form To:

Playmakers Press
c/o CMI Fulfillment
13518 L St., Omaha, NE 68137
E-mail: playmakers@conciergemarketing.com
Or order online at: *www.ThePlaymakers.org*

Authors (Top to Bottom): Greg Roeszler, Donna Miesbach, and David Humm

About the Authors

Greg Roeszler's passion for lost and forgotten kids caused him to leave a successful career in the business sector so he could devote his life to working with at-risk kids. As Greg puts it, "I am a high school football coach, and a husband and dad struggling to be the man I have been called to be." Out of that calling, Playmakers Mentoring Foundation was born. Supported early on by a network of coaches and friends who shared his vision, Playmakers currently reaches throughout the State of California, and has chapters in others cities around the country.

Greg, his wife, Linda, and their two daughters live in Sacramento, California.

For more information about Playmakers, please go to www.theplaymakers.org.

Donna Miesbach co-authored both of the Playmakers' books. Her award-winning book, *From Grief to Joy: A Journey Back to Life & Living*, is available through her web site (donnamiesbach.com) as well as amazon.com, libraries, and book stores. Her collection of poems, *Trails of Stardust, Poems of Inspiration and Insight*, was published in 2002. Some of her poems have also been published as choral anthems.

Her inspirational poems and articles reach around the globe through such venues as *Unity Magazine, Daily Word, Contemplative Journal*, and the *Chicken Soup* series. In 1985, Donna was named "Inspirational Poet of the Year" by *The Poet Magazine*.

Ms. Miesbach is a certified Chopra Center meditation and yoga instructor and has an active teaching practice which reaches into several Midwestern States.

She is a retired organist and resides in Omaha, Nebraska.

David Humm knows football like the back of his hand. More than that, he knows what it takes to be a quality player, both on and off the field. David was one of Nebraska University's most outstanding quarterbacks, setting records from 1972-74 that still have not been broken.

After receiving numerous prestigious awards, he spent the next ten years in the NFL where he played for the Oakland/LA Raiders, the Buffalo Bills, and the Baltimore Colts. It was as a Raider that David and his team won the Super Bowl XXI and Super Bowl XVIII Championships.

For the last twenty-one seasons, Hummer has been the co-host of the Oakland Raiders pre-game and post-game shows for the Oakland Raiders Radio Network. He is affectionately known by millions as one of the Voices of the Raiders Radio Broadcasts.

David lives and works in Las Vegas, Nevada.

www.ingramcontent.com/pod-product-compliance
Lightning Source LLC
Chambersburg PA
CBHW051708040426
42446CB00008B/783